TICKET TO THE

T0102602

TENNIS
GRAND SLAM

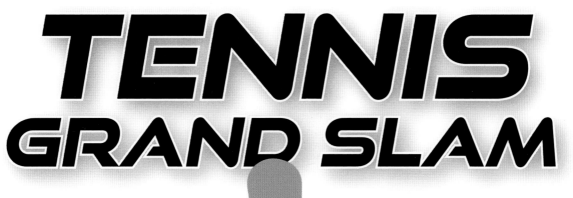

MARTIN GITLIN

45TH PARALLEL PRESS

Published in the United States of America by Cherry Lake Publishing Group
Ann Arbor, Michigan
www.cherrylakepublishing.com

Reading Adviser: Beth Walker Gambro, MS Ed., Reading Consultant, Yorkville, IL
Book Designer: Jen Wahi

Photo Credits: Cover: © photoyh/Shutterstock; page 5: © Neale Cousland/Shutterstock; page 7: © Alison Young/
Shutterstock; page 9: © Zhukovsky/Dreamstime.com; page 11: © Jerry Coli/Dreamstime.com; page 12: © Zairbek
Mansurov/Dreamstime.com; page 17: © Stuart Slavicky/Shutterstock; page 19: © Sports Images/Dreamstime.com; page 23:
© Jerry Coli/Dreamstime.com; page 25: © lev radin/Shutterstock; page 27: © Zhukovsky/Dreamstime.com; page 28 (top):
© Neale Cousland/Shutterstock; page 28 (bottom): © lev radin/Shutterstock

45th Parallel Press is an imprint of Cherry Lake Publishing Group.

Library of Congress Cataloging-in-Publication Data

Names: Gitlin, Marty, author.
Title: Ticket to the Tennis Grand Slam : the big game / Written by: Martin
  Gitlin.
Description: Ann Arbor, Michigan : Cherry Lake Publishing, [2023] | Series:
  The big game | Audience: Grades 4-6 | Summary: "Who has won the Tennis
  Grand Slam? How did they make it to the finals? Written as high interest
  with struggling readers in mind, this series includes considerate
  vocabulary, engaging content and fascinating facts, clear text and
  formatting, and compelling photos. Educational sidebars include extra
  fun facts and information about each championship. Includes table of
  contents, glossary, index, and author biography"-- Provided by
  publisher.
Identifiers: LCCN 2022039912 | ISBN 9781668919514 (hardcover) | ISBN
  9781668920534 (paperback) | ISBN 9781668923191 (pdf) | ISBN
  9781668921869 (ebook)
Subjects: LCSH: Tennis--Tournaments--Juvenile literature. |
  Tennis--Miscellanea--Juvenile literature.
Classification: LCC GV999 .G58 2023 | DDC 796.342--dc23/eng/20220819
LC record available at https://lccn.loc.gov/2022039912

Cherry Lake Publishing would like to acknowledge the work of the Partnership for 21st Century Learning, a network of
Battelle for Kids. Please visit http://www.battelleforkids.org/networks/p21

Printed in the United States of America
Corporate Graphics

Table of Contents

Introduction

The best tennis players compete nearly all year. They play tournaments. Those are a series of matches. The winners advance to the next round. The last winner is the champion.

The men play against men. The women play against women. Some tournaments have both men's and women's events. Other times they play different tournaments. They are held all around the world.

A tennis match is made up of games and sets. A player must win 4 points to win a game. The first to win 6 games takes the set. Women must win 2 sets to win a match. Men must win 3.

Players cannot win by 1 point or game. They must win by 2 in both cases. They can win a set by a 6–4 score. But they cannot win 6–5.

Serena Williams plays at the Australian Open tennis tournament in Melbourne, Australia.

Sets tied at 6–6 are decided by a tiebreaker. Those are a series of points played to decide a winner.

Top players compete all year. But 4 events are most important. They are Grand Slam events. They get the most interest. The best players compete in every Grand Slam event. Each event lasts 2 weeks.

The first is the Australian Open. It is held in January. Australians are known for loving tennis. Some of the world's best players came from Australia.

The French Open is next. It runs from late May to early June. The French Open is played on clay courts. Courts are the surface on which tennis is played. Some pros play better on clay. The balls bounce slower.

Wimbledon is an event held in England. It is the third Grand Slam event. It is also the most famous. It is played in July on grass courts. Many believe Wimbledon is the biggest event in tennis.

The U.S. Open is the last Grand Slam event. It is held in August and September. The event is played in Flushing, New York. That town is near New York City.

Spain's Rafael Nadal prepares to hit the ball in a game at Wimbledon. Wimbledon is a tournament held in London, England.

Best of the Best

It was 1932. The U.S. Open final was about to begin. Jack Crawford and Fred Perry were playing for the title.

Crawford had already won the Australian Open and the French Open. He had also won Wimbledon.

New York Times writer John Kieran took notice. He wrote that Crawford could win the Grand Slam events. It was the first time the term was used for tennis.

Crawford lost to Perry. But Kieran had made history. The 4 events are forever known as the Grand Slam events.

A Grand Slam also means winning all 4 titles in 1 year. It is very rare. Only 2 men have done it in singles. U.S. player Don Budge was the first in 1938.

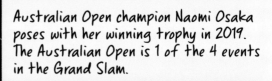

Australian Open champion Naomi Osaka poses with her winning trophy in 2019. The Australian Open is 1 of the 4 events in the Grand Slam.

Rod Laver was even better. Laver was from Australia. He is one of the greatest players ever. He is the only player to win the Grand Slam twice. Laver swept all 4 events in 1962 and 1969.

Three women have won Grand Slams. It was also done first by an American. It was done second by an Australian. U.S. player Maureen Connolly won all 4 events in 1953. Then Margaret Court of Australia did it in 1970.

The third was Steffi Graf of Germany. She captured a Grand Slam in 1988.

Most of the best players never won a Grand Slam. But they won many Grand Slam events.

Some took 3 of 4 in the same year. Two men won the first 3 events of the year. Then they lost the U.S. Open. Jack Crawford was the first. Lew Hoad also just missed in 1956.

This also happened to 1 woman. That was American Serena Williams in 2015.

Martina Navratilova twice won 3 Grand Slam events. She lost only 1 in 1983 and 1984. Many feel she was the best female player ever.

Some people think Martina Navratilova is the best female tennis player ever.

Players have often fallen 1 win short. They include the greatest in tennis history. Among them was Roger Federer. He is from Switzerland.

Federer won 3 Grand Slam events in 2004, 2006, and 2007. He is perhaps the best male player of all time.

Others believe the greatest were Federer's rivals. A rival is a person who competes with someone to be the best. One was Rafael Nadal of Spain. He won 3 of 4 Grand Slam events in 2010.

Roger Federer won the men's singles at the 2007 U.S. Open. This was the fourth time in a row!

France once ruled men's tennis. Its players won many Grand Slam events in the 1920s and 1930s.

The 4 best were called the Four Musketeers. They combined to win 20 titles. The top 2 were René Lacoste and Henri Cochet.

Lacoste was ranked No. 1 in the world for 2 years. Cochet was ranked No. 1 from 1928 to 1931.

WAY BACK WHEN

Nadal played his best at the French Open. He enjoyed an amazing run there. Nadal won it 14 times from 2005 to 2022.

Another great rival of Federer and Nadal was Novak Djokovic from Serbia. Djokovic won 3 Grand Slam events in 2011, 2015, and 2021.

The best women's player of the 2000s? There is no debate. It was Serena Williams. She won an amazing 23 Grand Slam events from 1999 to 2017.

Williams came from a tennis-playing family. Her sister Venus won 5 Wimbledon titles. She also took U.S. Open titles in 2000 and 2001.

Only 1 woman won more than Serena Williams. And that was Margaret Court. She won 24 Grand Slam events. She played her best in her home country of Australia. Court took every Australian Open from 1960 to 1966. She then won 4 more.

In the 1970s, an American replaced Court as the best in the world. She was teenager Chris Evert.

Evert was an amazing player. She often hit many shots in a row without missing. That upset opponents. Evert won 18 Grand Slam titles. Her best event was the French Open. She won 7 from 1974 to 1986.

American men fell behind after 2003. None won any Grand Slam event through 2021. But Americans did well in men's tennis before that.

 Among them was Jimmy Connors. He won 8 Grand Slam events from 1974 to 1983.

 Another was John McEnroe. He took 7 Grand Slam events from 1979 to 1984.

 Two American men dominated the 1990s and beyond. They were Pete Sampras and Andre Agassi.

 Sampras was often No. 1 in the world. He was top-ranked every year from 1993 to 1998. He won 14 Grand Slam events. Agassi won 8.

A BIT OF TRIVIA

Great Grand Slam Moments

It was easy to pick the best men's players in 2008. One was Federer. The other was Nadal. The 2 greats met in the 2008 Wimbledon final.

Federer had won the last 5 Wimbledon titles. He had beaten Nadal for the 2007 title. But Nadal was a rising star.

The fans were in for a treat. They saw perhaps the greatest match ever.

The clash lasted nearly 5 hours. Nadal won the first 2 sets. Federer battled back to take the third.

Nadal forged ahead in the fourth set. He gained match point. That means he needed to win 1 more point to take the match. But Federer won it to stay alive. Again Nadal had match point. Federer won that too. And he captured the set.

Federer serves the ball at Wimbledon.

The battle went down to a fifth set. The winner would be Wimbledon champion. Federer and Nadal kept on battling. Wimbledon matches cannot be decided by a tiebreaker.

The two were tied at 6–6. Then 7–7. Nadal finally broke through. He won the set 9–7. Somebody had finally beaten Federer at Wimbledon.

John McEnroe called it the greatest tennis match ever. And that meant a lot. In the 1980 Wimbledon final, McEnroe played Björn Borg of Sweden for the title.

McEnroe and Borg had different styles. McEnroe liked to rush to the net. He tried to win by hitting volleys. Those are shots players hit before they bounce.

Borg stayed on the baseline. That is the back line of the court. He had amazing ground strokes. Those are shots players hit after the ball bounces.

Borg and McEnroe were opposites in other ways. McEnroe was intense. He had a bad temper on the court. Borg was always calm. It seemed nothing ever bothered him.

Björn Borg prepares his backhand.

McEnroe won the first set easily. Borg took the next 2. The fourth set was tied at 6–6. It had to be decided by a tiebreaker. And it was perhaps the greatest tiebreaker in tennis history.

The 2 stars battled on and on. Tiebreakers must be won by at least 2 points. McEnroe finally won it 18–16.

The match was not over. Borg won a thrilling fifth set. He had snagged another Wimbledon title.

It was the first round of Wimbledon in 2010. U.S. player John Isner was about to play Nicolas Mahut of France.

What followed was amazing. It was the longest match in tennis history.

The first 4 sets were not unusual. Both players won 2 of them. Then came the fifth set. The men battled to a 6–6 tie.

There are no fifth-set tiebreakers at Wimbledon. So Isner and Mahut played on. They kept going and going. Neither could take a 2-game lead needed to win.

The fifth set lasted more than 8 hours. It had to be finished the next day. Isner finally won it 70–68. He and Mahut played 183 games during those 2 days.

AMAZING MOMENT

A Rich Rivalry

Women have also played incredible Grand Slam matches. Perhaps the best was the 1985 French Open final between Chris Evert and Martina Navratilova.

They were great rivals. They had already played each other 64 times. Navratilova had won 33. Evert had won 31. But no match was as amazing as that one.

The 2 had very different styles. Navratilova hit the ball hard. She often came to the net. She wanted to smash volleys to win points.

Evert stayed on the baseline. She tried to make shot after shot. Evert did not hit many winners. Those are shots other players cannot touch with their rackets. Evert was a different kind of player. She worked from the baseline to make her opponents miss.

Chris Evert is known as a tennis legend. Martina Navratilova was her biggest rival.

Evert seemed set to win easily. She won the first set. She was leading the second set 4–2. But Navratilova fought back. She won 4 straight games to take the set.

The third set was exciting. Evert led 5–3. Navratilova tied it at 5–5. She needed 1 point to win the next game. But Evert stopped her to go ahead 6–5. She then won the next game. That gave Evert the French Open title.

Martina Navratilova and Chris Evert unite to celebrate Serena Williams. This photo was taken at her U.S. Open win in 2014.

Young Talent

Evert and Navratilova were all-time greats. But some feel Serbian Monica Seles was better. Her 1992 French Open final was amazing.

Seles was ranked No. 1 in the world. She had won her first Grand Slam event at age 16. She staged an epic battle against Steffi Graf. Graf was ranked second.

The stars split the first 2 sets. Graf was about to lose the third. But she saved 5 match points to stay alive. She rallied to take a 6–5 lead.

The pair battled on. Seles finally won the set 10–8. It was already her sixth Grand Slam event title. And she was only 18.

Another well-known young talent is Naomi Osaka of Japan.

Gaël Monfils is another big tennis star! He is from France. Here he is playing at the 2012 Australian Open.

Sloane Stephens is an American tennis player who won the 2017 U.S. Open.

★ Australia ruled men's tennis for 20 years. This lasted from the 1950s into the 1970s.

★ The first star was Ken Rosewall. He had an amazing career. He won his first Grand Slam event in 1953. He was 18 years old. He won his last in 1972 at age 37.

★ The next champ was Roy Emerson. He won every Australian Open from 1965 to 1967.

★ Rod Laver might have been the best. He twice swept all 4 Grand Slam events. He is the only player to do that.

★ John Newcombe was another amazing Australian. He won 7 Grand Slam tournaments from 1967 to 1975.

LEGENDS OF THE SPORT

Activity

Tennis is great exercise. Play tennis with a friend or family member. See if you enjoy it. Keep trying to improve. You might take tennis lessons. Try to get more friends to play tennis with you. Find other sports that can keep you active.

Learn More

BOOKS

Buckley, James Jr. *Who Are Serena and Venus Williams?* New York: Penguin Workshop, 2017.

Hubbard, Crystal. *The Story of Tennis Champion Arthur Ashe.* New York: Lee & Low Books, 2018.

Pollman, Valerie R. *The Big Book of Tennis Facts: For Kids and Adults.* Independently published, 2018.

WEBSITES

Elite Sports Clubs: Tennis Fun Facts: https://eliteclubs.com/tennis-fun-facts/

Play Your Court: Find Kids' Tennis Lessons Near You: https://www.playyourcourt.com/kids-tennis-lessons/

Tennis for Kids Quiz: https://www.funtrivia.com/trivia-quiz/ForChildren/Tennis-for-Kids-389560.html

Glossary

baseline (BAYS-lyn) back line of a tennis court

courts (KORTS) surfaces on which tennis matches are played

ground strokes (GROWND STROHKZ) shots hit on a bounce

match point (MACH POYNT) point on which a player can win a match if won

rivals (RYE-vuhlz) people who compete with each other to be the best

tiebreaker (TY-bray-kuhr) series of points to decide the winner of a set or match

tournaments (TUR-nuh-muhnts) tennis events with a series of matches to decide a champion

volleys (VAH-leez) shots hit before the ball bounces, usually near the net

winners (WIH-nuhrs) shots in which the ball is not touched by an opponent

Index

About the Author

Marty Gitlin is a sports book author based in Cleveland. He won more than 45 awards as a newspaper sportswriter from 1991 to 2002. Included was a first-place award from the Associated Press for his coverage of the 1995 World Series. He has had more than 200 books published since 2006. Most of them were written for students.